W9-ATF-084

CRA

977.2
CRA
Craats, Rennay
Indiana

# INDIANA

**Rennay Craats**

Published by Weigl Publishers Inc.
123 South Broad Street, Box 227
Mankato, MN  56002
USA
Web site: http://www.weigl.com

Library of Congress Cataloging-in-Publication Data available upon request from the publisher. Fax: (507) 388-2746 for the attention of the Publishing Records Department.

ISBN 1-930954-65-4

Printed in the United States of America
1 2 3 4 5 6 7 8 9 10   05 04 03 02 01

**Project Coordinators**
Rennay Craats
Michael Lowry
**Substantive Editor**
Carlotta Lemieux
**Copy Editors**
Heather Kissock
Jennifer Nault
**Designers**
Warren Clark
Terry Paulhus
**Photo Researcher**
Jennifer Nault

**Photograph Credits**

Every reasonable effort has been made to trace ownership and to obtain permission to reprint copyright material. The publishers would be pleased to have any errors or omissions brought to their attention so that they may be corrected in subsequent printings.

Cover: Racecars (Indianapolis Motor Speedway), Limestone (Corel Corporation); Archive Photos: pages 18, 21, 24, 25; Children's Museum of Indianapolis: page 24; Corel Corporation: pages 11, 13, 14; Digital Stock: page 15; Dubois County Tourism: page 23; Eiteljorg Museum: page 16; Elkhart County Convention and Visitors Bureau: page 22; Eyewire Corporation: page 13; Charlene Faris: pages 16, 18, 19, 24; Globe Photos: pages 3, 25, 26, 27; Holiday World, Indiana: page 29; Indianapolis Convention and Visitors Bureau: page 20; Indiana Department of Commerce: pages 12, 20, 21; Indiana Department of Natural Resources: pages 3, 4, 5, 6, 7, 8, 9, 10, 11, 14, 15, 20, 21, 22, 28; Indianapolis Motor Speedway: pages 12, 26; Indiana State Library: pages 7, 19, 29; Perdue University: page 28; University of Texas, Institute of Texan Cultures: page 17; Wisconsin Historical Society: page 18.

# CONTENTS

# INTRODUCTION

Indiana is well known by its nickname–the "Hoosier State." In fact, the Hoosier State is the most famous of all the United States' nicknames. Indiana is also the home of the popular Indianapolis 500 car race. Equally interesting are the people, industry, sports, entertainment, and history of the state. This fascinating midwestern state is full of surprises. Indiana has lush forest areas and beautiful beaches along the shores of Lake Michigan. There is unlimited fun to be found in the sand dunes that line the lake area. Millions of tourists flock to Indiana to visit all of the wonderful attractions and the breathtaking scenery.

The Chain O'Lakes State Park is one example of Indiana's spectacular recreational areas.

The Feast of the Hunters' Moon festival is a celebration of Indiana's Native American heritage.

## QUICK FACTS

**Indiana was the** nineteenth state to enter the Union.

**The tulip tree** is Indiana's state tree.

**The state motto** is "**Crossroads** of America," because of its location in central United States. The motto was adopted in 1937.

Downtown Terre Haute can be a confusing place, with roads branching off in all directions.

## Getting There

Of all the prairie states, Indiana is the farthest east. It occupies the smallest area of all the midwestern states. Indiana is bordered by Michigan to the north, Ohio to the east, Illinois to the west, and Kentucky to the south. People often travel Indiana's many highways on their way to the coasts. It really is the "crossroads" of the nation. To help traffic into and out of Indiana, the state has 92,000 miles of road.

Passenger trains make regular stops in close to twenty cities in the state. People who enjoy air travel can fly to the Indianapolis International Airport or to the many other airports in Indiana. There are more than 130 public airports in the state and many small, private airstrips. Visitors to Indiana can also reach it by boat. The state's busiest **port** is Portage's Burns Waterway Harbor.

## QUICK FACTS

**Including inland water**, Indiana spans 36,420 square miles.

**The official flower** was originally the carnation. People objected because the carnation is a European flower. The official flower was later changed to the tulip tree blossom, the zinnia, and the dogwood blossom before the peony became the official flower in 1957.

**Indiana's state song** is "On the Banks of the Wabash, Far Away."

### Location Map

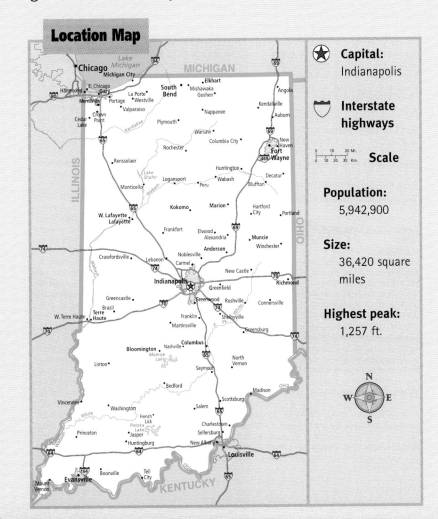

⭐ **Capital:** Indianapolis

🛡 **Interstate highways**

**Scale**

**Population:** 5,942,900

**Size:** 36,420 square miles

**Highest peak:** 1,257 ft.

Indiana may be a confusing state to outsiders. The towns of Center, Center Square, and Centerville are not even located in the middle of the state. The city of South Bend is really one of the state's most northerly cities. North Vernon, on the other hand, is close to the Ohio River on Indiana's southern border. West College Corner is located on the state's eastern border, and East Mt. Carmel stands on the southwestern corner of Indiana. The state is also home to three Georgetowns, three Jamestowns, four Millersburgs, five Mt. Pleasants, two Klondykes, and one Klondike. These little quirks only add to the appeal of the Hoosier State.

**The cardinal, a North American songbird, feeds on wild seeds, fruits, and insects.**

**Holiday lights illuminate Washington Street in Indianapolis.**

## QUICK FACTS

**The cardinal** is Indiana's state bird. It is also the state bird of six other states.

**The Wabash River** is Indiana's official state river. It was adopted in 1996. Indiana is one of the few states that has a river as an official symbol.

**Indiana means** "Home of the Indians." The name is a reference to the Native Americans that lived in the region.

The drastically different regions of Indiana mean that the state has a variety of climates. Indiana is generally a humid state. The waters of Lake Michigan in the north heat the region during winter and cool it down during summer. Winter temperatures are higher in this region. The numerous hills, valleys, and forests across the southern parts of Indiana cause the temperature to differ from region to region.

Limestone **quarries** can be found in southern Indiana. Craftsmen use limestone as a building stone.

Many of the sand dunes in Indiana were formed by westerly winds. The winds carried sand from bare fields and deposited it on the shores of northern lowland lakes.

## QUICK FACTS

**Indiana's state flag**
is blue with nineteen gold stars that surround a flaming torch. The five stars closest to the torch represent the states that entered the Union before Indiana. The other thirteen stars in the outer circle represent the original states. The last star, representing Indiana, is right above the torch. The word "Indiana" is placed in a half circle above the torch.

**Santa Claus, Indiana,**
receives more than 500,000 letters from children at Christmas time.

# LAND AND CLIMATE

**Wyandotte Cave has 23 miles of passages and several large open chambers.**

The Great Lakes area is known as Indiana's lowlands. There are many smaller lakes in this region as well. Most of Indiana's lowland lakes were formed by melting glaciers. To the south of the lowlands lies rich, dark soil that is ideal for farming.

Most agriculture takes place in central Indiana. The land here displays evidence of ancient glaciers. As the glaciers moved, they left behind layers of debris that had been trapped in the ice. The remaining debris provided proof to scientists of the glaciers' passing. While this region is fairly flat, there are some low hills and slight valleys.

Indiana has warm summers and cool winters. In the summer, the average temperature is 75 °Fahrenheit. The average temperature in winter drops to 28 °F. The state has had periods of dry weather as well as occasional floods. At times, Indiana experiences tornadoes.

**A major flood in 1997 drenched the town of Alton.**

## QUICK FACTS

**Monument Mountain** is in Wyandotte Cave. It is the highest underground mountain in the world.

**The southern region** of Indiana draws the most people, including tourists and residents.

**Indiana receives** around 40 inches of rain each year.

**Indiana's highest point** is Franklin Township at 1,257 feet. The lowest point is the Ohio River at 320 feet.

**The lowest recorded** temperature in Indiana was –35 °F in 1951. The highest temperature was a sweltering 116 °F in 1936.

**The lowlands are** home to sand dunes, a source of tourism and entertainment in Indiana.

BOAT
←RAMP

# NATURAL RESOURCES

One of Indiana's most valuable resources is its limestone. This limestone was formed nearly 300 million years ago when the area was still a shallow ocean bed. Small sea creatures died leaving their bones, which eventually hardened and piled up, creating limestone. Indiana has one of the biggest deposits of limestone in the world. The stone was used to build such landmarks as the Pentagon, the Empire State Building, and the Rockefeller Center.

With large forested areas, Indiana relies heavily on trees as an important resource. The forests provide timber that is sold throughout the state and the rest of the country. All over Indiana, sand and gravel are also valued resources. Coal is one of Indiana's most important minerals. It is mined in the southwestern regions of the state, and the richest mines are in Terre Haute. Other resources found in Indiana are natural gas and petroleum.

## QUICK FACTS

**Southern Indiana has** around 700 limestone caves. The most famous of these are Wyandotte, Marengo, and Bluesprings.

**Gypsum, a chalk-like** material, is found in the counties of La Porte, Owen, and Martin.

**The discovery of** natural gas in the 1880s created a **boom** in Indiana.

**Powerful digging machines called draglines are used in strip-mining.**

# PLANTS AND ANIMALS

Almost one-sixth of Indiana is covered in forests. Many different kinds of trees are found here, including black walnut, hickory, oak, and maple. Along the Ohio River, bald cypress, black tupelo, cottonwood, and Virginia pines flourish.

The moist, shady areas of Indiana are home to prickly-pear cacti, irises, and orchids. Insects have to beware of some of Indiana's plants. The bladderwort, pitcher plant, and round-leaved sundew feast on insects along the north shores of the state. Several other plants bloom and fill the air with their sweet smells. Peonies, pussy willows, and violets all appear in the springtime, while oxeye daisies and corn cockle are seen during summer. Autumn in Indiana is the time for sunflowers, goldenrod, and asters.

## QUICK FACTS

**Before pioneers** arrived in Indiana, 80 percent of the state was covered in forests.

**More than 100** species of trees are native to Indiana. They include seventeen different kinds of oak.

**Other animals** living in Indiana include otters, beavers, and opposums.

**Sunflower petals** can be used to make yellow dye, and their seeds make a healthy cooking oil or a tasty treat.

**Indiana has many** wild turkeys and pheasants.

**The sand dunes** in the north are home to more than 3,000 kinds of plants and bush.

**The Hoosier National Forest** draws nature lovers and hikers to explore its wonders.

The variety of land in Indiana makes it an ideal home for many different kinds of animals. Deer, muskrats, rabbits, raccoons, skunks, and woodchucks live in the state's forests and prairies. Red foxes are one of the most common **carnivores** in the state. Some of Indiana's animals have become **endangered**. The badger and the bobcat still live in Indiana, but are rarely seen anymore.

Indiana's lakes, rivers, and streams hold many bass, catfish, pike, salmon, and sunfish. Along the shores of Indiana's northern lakes, black ducks and great blue herons make their homes. Yellow-winged sparrows and prairie larks can be found in the prairies close to swampy areas. Birdwatchers can spot cardinals, blue jays, orioles, and wrens flying in Indiana's skies.

**The red fox has a remarkable sense of smell that helps it avoid natural predators and hunters.**

# TOURISM

The Conner Prairie Pioneer Settlement shows tourists what life was like in the 1880s.

There is a great deal to do in Indiana. For history buffs, Fort Wayne offers a peek into the past. It was built at the site of a Miami Native American village. At the rebuilt Fort Wayne, uniformed soldiers carry out military activities of that time period. Another historical attraction is the Conner Prairie Pioneer Settlement in Noblesville. It includes an old log cabin that was once used as a trading post.

Indiana's landscape draws tourists from all over the world. Both nature-lovers and tourists flock to explore the limestone caves and underground caverns in the south. Other visitors travel to northern Indiana to visit the sand dunes. These natural wonders line the shores of the Great Lakes.

Indiana's largest tourist attraction is the world-famous Indianapolis Motor Speedway. The Indianapolis 500 is held there once a year in May. More than 300,000 people gather in Indianapolis to watch this race.

**The Indianapolis Motor Speedway was once paved with 3.2 million bricks, earning it the nickname "The Brickyard." The bricks have since been paved over with asphalt.**

## QUICK FACTS

**The Conner Prairie Pioneer Settlement** showcases the mansion of famous pioneer William Conner.

**People visit** Parke county for its covered bridges. There are more than thirty. The bridge over Sugar Creek is 207 feet long. It is the longest single-span covered bridge in the United States.

**The Indianapolis Motor Speedway** has more than 250,000 permanent seats, making it the world's largest seating facility.

Welders must wear protective clothing when they are working.

# INDUSTRY

Indiana's manufactured products are important to its economy. Steel is the most important metal that the state produces. Indiana makes more steel than any other state in the country. Burns Harbor and Gary are Indiana's major steel-producing centers. Bedford, Lafayette, and Newburgh are also important industrial cities. They are producers of aluminum.

**Pharmaceuticals** are another important product. Eli Lilly is a major pharmaceutical company with its business base in Indianapolis.

Other Indiana industries include the **manufacturing** of electrical equipment such as electrical car parts, radios, televisions, and appliances. Delco Electronics, which developed the push-button car radio and the all-transistor car radio, has its headquarters in Kokomo. The state also makes engines, machine tools, and refrigeration equipment.

## QUICK FACTS

**The Calumet region** is one of the world's major steel-producing areas. It is located in the northwestern part of the state.

**Plastic products** are made in several Indiana cities.

**Baked goods,** dairy products, meats, and soft drinks make up the bulk of Indiana's food production.

Medicines created by pharmaceutical companies help people live longer, healthier lives.

# GOODS AND SERVICES

Farmland takes up approximately 70 percent of the state's land. There are close to 63,000 farms spread out across the state. Two of Indiana's most important crops are corn and soybeans. Together, these two crops bring in nearly half the total farming income each year. Other crops in the state include hay and wheat.

Transportation equipment, especially vehicle and aircraft parts, make up a large part of Indiana's manufactured goods. Indiana is one of the leading states in the production of automobile parts, truck and bus bodies, trailers, and motor homes.

**Farming has been an important activity in Indiana since the state's early days.**

## QUICK FACTS

**Hogs are Indiana's** leading livestock product. Some other major livestock products are milk, beef, and eggs.

**Manufacturing employs** more people than any other industry in Indiana.

**A new Blueberry Queen is crowned every year in Plymouth.**

Apples, blueberries, and watermelons are the state's leading fruit crops. Farmers also harvest cucumbers, onions, and potatoes. Movie buffs can thank Indiana for their treats—the state ranks second in the nation in popcorn production.

The service industry is very important to Indiana. It consists of people who do things for other people—this includes occupations ranging from doctors to bus drivers. Other service people wait on tables, operate rides at amusement parks, or take reservations at hotels. The hotel business is especially important in Indiana because of the large number of conventions held in Indianapolis.

To keep informed, Indianans can pick up one of the 300 newspapers or 170 magazines that are published throughout the state. The biggest newspaper in the state is the *Indianapolis Star*.

**Indiana's popcorn sales are best in the fall. Fewer people munch on popcorn in the summer.**

# FIRST NATIONS

When the first explorers arrived in Indiana in the 1600s, they encountered as few as one hundred First Nations peoples. Most early First Nations peoples were from the Miami Nation. In the 1700s, the fur trade caused bloody conflicts between the Europeans and the First Nations peoples, including the Wea, Potawatomi, Kickapoo, and Piankashaw. Other groups, including the Delaware, Munsee, and Shawnee, arrived in Indiana after wars with the Europeans had driven them from their homes along the Atlantic coast.

The Miami Nation were among the first groups to put down roots in the Indiana area. They stayed in central and northern Indiana for approximately 150 years. The Miami built houses by covering poles in the ground with bark and cattail mats. They planted crops of pumpkins, beans, and corn. The Potawatomi were the last Native Americans to enter and then leave Indiana. They lived in the northern part of the state.

**QUICK FACTS**

**The Eiteljorg Museum** of American Indian and Western Art is in a building that looks like a Native American **pueblo**. The building is as much a work of art as the pieces inside the museum.

**Indiana's first** inhabitants were nomadic hunters who lived in the area as early as 12,000 years ago.

**Miami chief** Little Turtle fought using a combination of European and Native American tactics. He used European combat maneuvers along with his ability to move quickly through wilderness areas.

The Eiteljorg Museum in downtown Indianapolis houses Native American art and artifacts.

# EXPLORERS AND MISSIONARIES

**René-Robert Cavelier led the first European quest to track the Mississippi River to the Gulf of Mexico.**

French explorer René-Robert Cavelier, the Sieur de La Salle, is believed to have been the first European to visit Indiana. He came from New France, a French colony on the St. Lawrence River. La Salle claimed a great deal of midwestern North America for France.

La Salle passed through the state in 1679 and returned two years later. He traveled the St. Joseph River, reaching the area now known as South Bend. La Salle tried to encourage the Miami and their neighbors, the Illinois, to stand up against the Iroquois. The Iroquois were powerful **allies** of the British, and La Salle wanted to block the British fur trade and encourage the French trade. He was unsuccessful in convincing the two groups, but he still claimed the area for France.

A handful of dedicated French priests risked their lives in an attempt to spread Christianity to the Native Americans. Many Jesuit priests led the charge into the wilderness of Indiana.

**Jesuit priests played an important role in the colonization of midwestern American regions.**

# EARLY SETTLERS

After La Salle and many other Frenchmen claimed the Great Lakes area for New France, settlements began to spring up. The rivers were used as highways and forts were built along the shoreline during the 1700s. Fort Ouiatenon, Fort Miami, Fort Wayne, and Fort Vincennes were Indiana's first permanent settlements. It was not long before small villages sprouted up outside the forts' walls. These villages were under French rule, even though less than 3 percent of the population were French.

The British were also exploring and settling in North America and were often at war with the French. After the French and Indian War of 1763, the French gave up their claim to the Great Lakes region, which was taken over by Britain. The French and Native Americans had enjoyed a relationship of equals, but when the British took over, the relationship soured. Over time, the Native Americans came to dislike the British and conflicts between the two groups were common.

**Many settlers made their living off the fur trade.**

**The French and Indian War began as a fight between the French and the English over control of the upper Ohio River Valley. Four years later, the British claimed victory on the Plains of Abraham.**

**QUICK FACTS**

**In 1795,** the Miami Nation signed a treaty with the United States, handing over the majority of their land.

**By 1815,** around 60,000 pioneers lived in Indiana.

**Most of Indiana's** settlements developed without much planning. Indianapolis, on the other hand, was a planned city from the beginning. Indianapolis was actually modeled after the nation's capital – Washington, D.C.

In 1783, the United States won the Revolutionary War against the British. Following this victory, the first wave of American settlers came to Indiana from the southern states, including Kentucky, Virginia, and North and South Carolina. Nearly 20,000 more Americans sailed down the Ohio River to find land. These settlers built villages and planted crops in the southern part of the state. In the north, settlers from New York, Pennsylvania, and the New England states were also establishing settlements. Much later, a smaller group of settlers arrived from Europe and called Indiana their new home.

**Religious groups from Europe came to the United States looking for freedom. Religious settlements can still be found throughout the United States, and a large number of these settlements are in Indiana.**

# POPULATION

Indiana is the fourteenth most populated state in the United States. It has more than 5.9 million people living within its borders. The majority of people live in urban areas. One-third of Indianans live in the **metropolitan** areas of Gary and Indianapolis. Another heavily populated area is the northern region around Lake Michigan, also known as the Calumet region.

Five of the state's cities boast a population of more than one hundred thousand. Indianapolis is the largest city followed by Fort Wayne, Evansville, Gary, and South Bend. Indiana does not have one main city center that controls the culture and economy of the state. Instead, the culture of Indiana is spread throughout the major cities.

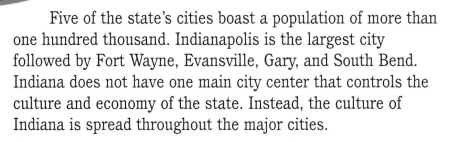

**Indianapolis is one of the most populated inland cities in the world.**

# POLITICS AND GOVERNMENT

Indianapolis's city center is almost entirely made up of government buildings. As stated in Indiana's 1851 constitution, the state government is divided into three levels: the executive, the legislative, and the judicial. The executive branch, led by the state's elected governor, is responsible for making sure the laws are carried out.

The legislative branch is made up of two houses: the Senate and the House of Representatives. The Senate has 50 members and the House of Representatives has 100. This branch enacts new laws and changes old ones. Both houses need to agree on a new **bill** before it is sent to the governor for approval.

The judicial branch houses the court system. The Supreme Court, which is made up of five members, and the Court of Appeals, which is made up of twelve members, are the highest courts in the state. The judges on these courts all serve two-year terms. If a judge is voted in for a second term, he or she will then be permitted to serve for another ten years.

**The Indiana State Capitol in Indianapolis is built with the state's most valuable natural resource, limestone.**

Today, about 8 percent of Indiana's population is African American.

# CULTURAL GROUPS

In the early 1800s, many freed African-American slaves settled in Indiana. By the 1860s, many more came to Indiana's cities in search of jobs. Indianapolis's Indiana Avenue was the center of entertainment in the 1920s. The avenue has become a treasured symbol of pride for the African-American community of Indianapolis.

Indiana has large **Amish** and **Mennonite** communities in the northern farmlands. The Amish and Mennonite follow a form of Christianity which restricts the use of modern technologies in favor of a simpler life. It is common to see horse-drawn carriages driven by Amish men and women in the Indiana countryside. The carriages take the place of automobiles, which are forbidden in Amish communities.

**Even though the Amish do not use modern farming machinery, they are excellent farmers.**

## QUICK FACTS

**The Amish religion** is an offshoot of the Mennonite religion. The Mennonites were first established in Switzerland in the 1500s.

**The first permanent** African-American resident in Indiana was likely housekeeper Cheney Lively.

**The rich jazz** culture in Indiana can be traced to the African Americans who settled and lived there.

While the majority of today's Indianans were born in the United States, some 6 percent were born in other countries. Some Indianans are descended from immigrants, many of whom where originally from Europe. Some of the largest ethnic groups in Indiana include Irish, English, French, Dutch, and Polish. Germans also have a strong presence in Indiana, with German social clubs and cultural centers throughout the state.

Many of Indiana's cultural groups celebrate their heritage with festivals. For three days in June, South Bend hosts the Ethnic Festival. This festival attracts about 70,000 people who enjoy the international displays and cooking. South Bend is also host to the Grecian Festival and the Polish Dyngus Day.

**The German people of Jasper, Indiana, celebrate their culture during the Strassenfest festival. Strassenfest means "Street Festival."**

# ARTS AND ENTERTAINMENT

For music lovers, Indiana is the place to be. Jazz and ragtime music are popular throughout the state. These upbeat types of music have been a part of the Hoosier State since the early 1900s. Indiana is also home to more than thirty symphony orchestras and over thirty-five choral groups. The Indianapolis Symphony Orchestra performs in the beautifully restored Circle Theater.

There are many famous Hoosier composers, including Hoagy Carmichael, who wrote "Georgia on My Mind," and Cole Porter, who wrote the musicals *Kiss Me, Kate* and *Can-Can*. Indiana also produced one of the most popular musical families in history—the Jackson Five. Michael Jackson and his brothers and sisters entertained their neighbors before making it big in Motown.

**At the Children's Museum of Indianapolis, visitors can enjoy and participate in a full-scale archaeological dig.**

**Award-winning** cartoonist Jim Davis, creator of *Garfield*, calls Indiana his home.

**New Harmony** became the educational and cultural capital of the state's frontier during the 1820s.

**Late night talk show** host David Letterman was born in Indianapolis.

**Many great painters** came out of Indiana. The "Hoosier Group" of romantic landscape artists made an impact on the art world during the late 1800s and early 1900s.

**The rolling hills** of Indiana attract many artists to Brown County. They are eager to capture the beautiful colors on their canvases.

**Actor James Dean is famous for the rebellious young characters he played in the movies.**

Hollywood has Indiana to thank for some talented movie actors. The most notable is James Dean. He starred in the 1950s teenage classics *Rebel Without a Cause* and *East of Eden*. He died in a car accident when he was twenty-four years old. James Dean still maintains a huge following throughout the country. Another star was comedian, Red Skelton, who took Hollywood by storm in the 1940s with movies such as *The Fuller Brush Man* and *A Southern Yankee*.

Indiana has been home to many successful writers since the early 1800s. Modern successes include Kurt Vonnegut, Jr., Irving Leibowitz, and Jessamyn West. Vonnegut received great acclaim for his science fiction stories *Cat's Cradle* and *Slaughterhouse Five*. West's novel, *The Friendly Persuasion*, told the story of an Indiana **Quaker** community. More great writers have come out of Indiana than any other similarly sized state in the country.

**Kurt Vonnegut's famous novel, *Slaughterhouse Five*, was loosely based on his experiences in the U.S. Air Force during World War II.**

# SPORTS

When people think of Indiana they often think of the Indianapolis 500. Hundreds of thousands of people come to watch the race at the Indianapolis Motor Speedway Stadium. The Indianapolis 500 counts 200 laps, which translates to 500 miles of fast driving. Cars race around the track at more than 160 miles per hour, and the winner takes home more than $3 million in prize money.

There is much more to Indiana sports than race cars. The state's residents cheer on their professional sports teams, which include the Pacers of the National Basketball Association and the Colts of the National Football League. Both of these sports teams entertain fans with their talented players, including football running back Eric Dickerson and basketball greats Reggie Miller and George McGinnis.

**The track at the Indianapolis Motor Speedway is 2.5 miles long and occupies 559 acres of land.**

## QUICK FACTS

**The Indianapolis 500** car race has been held every year over the Memorial Day weekend since 1911. It is the largest one-day sporting event in the world.

**Indiana's Mark Spitz** won seven gold medals at the 1972 Olympics.

**The first professional** baseball game took place in Fort Wayne in 1871. Fort Wayne beat Cleveland 2-0.

**The National Collegiate** Athletic Association Hall of Champions is located in Indianapolis. It celebrates achievements in college and university sports.

**Reggie Miller,
who played for the
Indiana Pacers, was
drafted by the NBA
in 1987.**

Indiana's AAA and minor league
teams have been an incredible
success. The Central Hockey
League (CHL) hockey team, the
Indianapolis Ice, won the league
championships in 2000. The
NBA development team, the
Fort Wayne Fury, had six
of its players called up
to play in the NBA.
The Indianapolis
Indians are the farm
team for the Major
League Baseball team,
the Milwaukee Brewers.
The team was named
the best AAA baseball
team of the nineties.

Many of Indiana's college teams
have dominated their sports. For
most of the twentieth century, the
University of Notre Dame near
South Bend has had one of the
best football teams. It was home
to talented players including Joe
Montana, Allan Page, Paul Hornung,
and Tim Brown. Indiana University's
basketball program has watched the
explosions and successes of coach
Bobby Knight. He was known as much
for his temper as for his championship
teams. His temper finally led to his
dismissal in September 2000.

**Joe Montana is known as "The Comeback Kid"
because he made thirty-four fourth-quarter
comebacks while he played for the NFL.**

# Brain Teasers

## 1

Why is Lafayette's Purdue University important to the town?

**Answer:** Besides producing many astronauts and being the center of entertainment, Purdue University is also the city's largest employer.

## 2

### True or False?

The Battle of Corydon was the only Civil War battle waged in Indiana.

**Answer: True.** The battle took place on July 9, 1863. Members of the Harrison County Home Guard tried to slow General John Hunt Morgan's Confederate soldiers. They were hoping that Union soldiers would arrive and stop Morgan from marching through southern Indiana.

## 3

Why is Kokomo known as a city of firsts?

**Answer:** Kokomo boasts the first car in America, owned by Elwood Haynes in 1894; the first mechanical corn picker, owned by John Powell in the early 1920s; and the first canned tomato juice by the Kemp Brothers Canning Company in 1928.

## 4

How did Terre Haute get its name?

**Answer:** When French explorers arrived in the area, they did so using the Wabash River. "Terre Haute" means "high ground." The area is 50 feet above the river's high-water mark, so explorers were climbing up to higher ground from the river banks.

# 5

## Where would you expect to find Holiday World?

**Answer:** Holiday World is an attraction in Santa Claus, Indiana. It celebrates Christmas, of course, as well as the Fourth of July and Halloween. It also has amusement rides and games. There is a wax museum featuring fifty people who have helped shape the United States.

# 6

## How did Indianans become known as "Hoosiers?"

**Answer:** One theory says that it came from Samuel Hoosier, a contractor who liked to use workers from the state. But most people believe that the nickname came from a slang expression. "Who's yer?" was said instead of "Who's here?" Other theories draw from the slang word "husher," which is someone who can calm a fight or from "hoozer," meaning hill.

# 7

## List the following Indiana cities in order from south to north.

Terre Haute, South Bend, Kokomo, Indianapolis, North Vernon, Crawfordsville

**Answer:** North Vernon, Terre Haute, Indianapolis, Crawfordsville, Kokomo, South Bend

# 8

## TRUE OR FALSE?

New Harmony would not let girls and boys learn together in the same school.

**Answer:** False. The community was the first in the United States to teach boys and girls together.

# FOR MORE INFORMATION

## Books

Stein, Conrad. *America the Beautiful: Indiana*. Chicago: Children's Press, 1990.

Thomas, Phyllis. *Indiana: Off the Beaten Path*. Connecticut: Globe Pequot Press, 1995.

Gisler, Margaret. *Indiana Family Adventure Guide*. Connecticut: Globe Pequot Press, 1995.

## Web Sites

You can also go online and have a look at the following Web sites:

Indiana Tourism
http://www.enjoyindiana.com

Indianapolis Visitors Center
http://www.indygov.org/visitors.htm

50 States: Indiana
http://www.50states.com/indiana.htm

Indianapolis 500
http://www.indy500.com

Some Web sites stay current longer than others. To find other Indiana Web sites, enter search terms such as "Indiana," "Indiana Pacers," "Indianapolis 500," or any other topic you want to research.

# GLOSSARY

**allies:** two groups that join together against a common enemy

**Amish:** a conservative Christian group from North America; offshoot of the Mennonites

**bill:** a draft of a proposed law

**boom:** a period of success

**carnivores:** meat eaters

**colonization:** to settle new land

**crossroads:** a place where two or more roads meet

**endangered:** in danger of becoming extinct

**Jesuit:** a member of the Roman Catholic religious order

**manufacturing:** the production of goods by hand or machine

**Mennonite:** a conservative Christian religion founded in Switzerland in the 1500s

**metropolitan:** the characteristics of a large, busy city

**pharmaceuticals:** drugs used for medicine and sold in pharmacies

**port:** a harbor where goods are imported and exported

**pueblo:** a common dwelling of agricultural Native peoples

**Quaker:** a Christian religion that does not believe in war

**quarries:** large pits from which blocks of stone are mined